MAR 06 2002

W'

COMPUTER ANIMATION

From Start to Finish

Samuel G. Woods

Photographs by Gale Zucker

BLACKBIRCH PRESS, INC.

WOODBRIDGE, CONNECTICUT

W

Special Thanks
The author and the publisher would like to thank Jay Nilsen, Don LaForce, Gerardo Orioli, Erik Paynter, Chris Conway, Curt Ramm, and Ralph Guardiano for their generous help in putting this project together.

Published by Blackbirch Press, Inc.
260 Amity Road
Woodbridge, CT 06525

e-mail: staff@blackbirch.com
Web site: www.blackbirch.com

©2000 by Blackbirch Press, Inc.
First Edition

Printed in Singapore

10 9 8 7 6 5 4 3 2 1

Photo Credits: All photographs © Gale Zucker, except page 4: Courtesy Sonalysts Studios.

Images on cover, contents, pages 3, 9, 12 (drawing), 13–15, 17 (bottom), 18, 19, 21–23, 30, 32 (bottom) courtesy Sonalysts studios.

Library of Congress Cataloging-in-Publication Data
Woods, Samuel G.
Computer animation / Samuel G. Woods
    p. cm. — (Made in the U.S.A.)
    Includes index.
    Summary: Describes the process of making commercials, television programs, and movies using computer animation.
    ISBN 1-56711-396-6 (hardcover : alk. paper)
    1. Computer animation—Juvenile literature. [1. Computer animation.]
I. Title. II. Made in the U.S. A.
TR897.7.W66 2000
006.6'96—dc21
                           00-009022
                           CIP

Contents

A Creative Place	4
"Spirit Piece"	6
Creating a Story	8
Who Will Star?	10
Goats and Mules	12
Characters Come Alive	14
"Plotting" the Character	16
The Finished Storyboard	18
Special Sequences	21
Details, Textures, and Light	22
Adding Sound	24
Sound Effects	26
"Layers" of Sound	28
Final Touches	30
Glossary	32
For More Information	32
Index	32

If you have seen popular movies—such as Toy Story, Antz, A Bug's Life, and Toy Soldiers—you have witnessed the magic of computer animation. Many television commercials—especially for kid's toys and food products—also feature computer animation.

How do animators make things like toys and ordinary household objects come alive on the screen? And how do computers help to make animated characters speak and move with such realism?

A Creative Place

Sonalysts Studios in Connecticut is a media production facility. Television commercials are filmed here. So are major motion pictures and network news specials. Pop music superstars record albums here. And printed flyers, catalogs, and brochures are created for resorts, hotels, casinos, and amusement parks.

One of the specialties at Sonalysts is computer animation. In this department, a team of talented artists and animators produces projects of all sorts. Often, when they are given a job, the animators must create characters and stories from scratch.

Erik Paynter (left) and Gerardo Orioli are two of the computer animators at Sonalysts.

"Spirit Piece"

Recently, Sonalysts was asked to create a special "spirit piece" for the U.S. Navy Submarine Force. The Navy wanted the piece to run during a commercial break for the Army-Navy football game. Both the Army and the Navy were allowed to air "spirit pieces" that would inspire their team to win.

Producer Don LaForce (left) had to organize the "spirit piece" project with Jay Nilsen, head of the animation department.

Don and Jay "brainstorm" some ideas for a storyline.

The entire Navy piece needed to be 30 seconds long. And Sonalysts had only 5 weeks to complete the project. This sounds like a lot of time for something that only runs for 30 seconds, but there is a great deal of work involved. Right away, the producer and the head of the animation department set to work.

7

Creating a Story

The first step in creating a commercial—or even a movie or television show—is to create a story. To do this, writers may sit down with producers to discuss ideas. Producers are in charge of finding resources and materials that may be needed to do the job. They also oversee the budget and make sure each project is done without spending too much money.

Top: *Beginning to sketch ideas.*
Bottom: *The details of a story come together.*

8

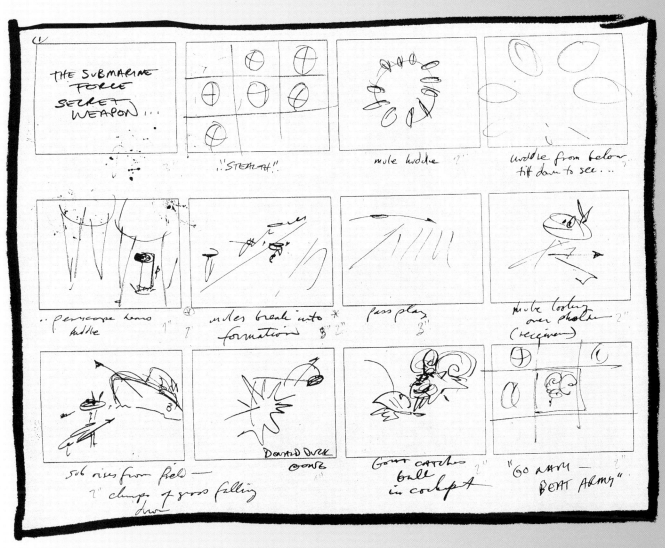

When a basic story is approved, a quick "visual outline" is created. This outline is a storyboard. A storyboard is a rough sketch of the action from beginning to end. This helps the animators to think of the story scene by scene.

Who Will Star?

Once the animators know what the basic story will involve, they can begin to create their main characters. For the Navy piece, there were two major groups of characters: the goats and the mules. The goat is the official mascot of the U.S. Navy. The mule is the official mascot for the U.S. Army. At Sonalysts, one animator was given the job of creating and animating the goats. Another animator was responsible for all the mules.

Erik and Gerardo begin their development of the mules and goats.

Above and right: The animators study reference material as they discuss their characters.

Every character begins with some basic sketches.

Goats and Mules

To create his goat characters, Gerardo did a lot of research. He looked at magazine articles and studied how other goat characters have been drawn. He also used the Navy's official mascot as the "foundation" for his creation. Gerardo decided he wanted his goats to look "clever" with a kind of "mischievous look" in their eyes. This would work well, because the goats in the piece are up to mischief.

Erik Paynter was in charge of creating the mules. He also did a great deal of research. Erik decided that he wanted to create mules that looked fairly realistic, but also had kind of "confused" expressions. The mules were the "bad guys" in the piece. In the end, they are tricked by the clever goats.

Top and bottom: Erik's initial sketches for his mule characters.

13

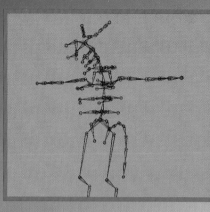

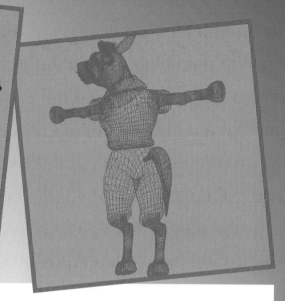

Characters Come Alive

Once their sketches were approved, the animators began creating the characters on the computer. Each character was created from head to toe. To do this, the animators must think about how each character's body is put together. This affects how the character moves, how it speaks, and what kinds of expressions it will make.

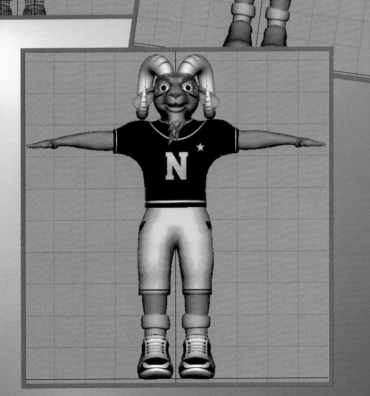

Both Erik and Gerardo have studied drawing and anatomy. These studies teach about how objects move, how lighting works, and how bodies are put together. They have also studied many animation software programs. "It's hard to say if computer animation is more art than technical skill," Gerardo says, "I would say it's about 50/50."

Opposite page and this page: *Each character is created with an interior "skeleton" that has many layers added to it.*

15

"Plotting" the Character

When the basic design of a character is complete, many details need to be filled in. Every point that will move on a character's body must be "plotted," or mapped, for the computer. The computer then figures out how all these points change as the characters move in space. This makes each character's movement and appearance realistic.

Erik plots the head of a mule on his machine.

Every character's body is made up of many different points. These points are laid out on a grid, which looks like a net. To make a character's body move, the animators tell the computer which points on the grid to move.

17

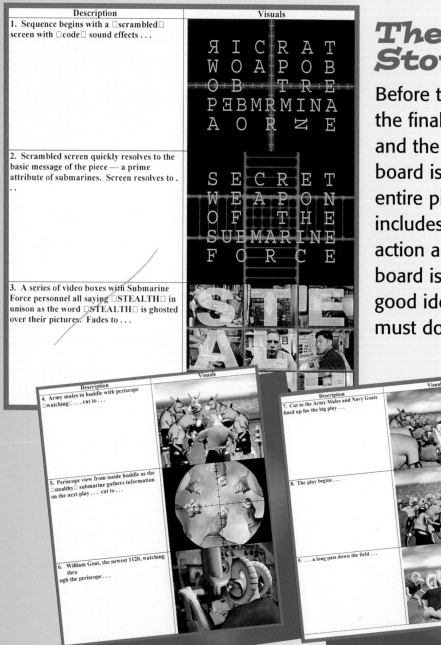

Description	Visuals
1. Sequence begins with a ▯scrambled▯ screen with ▯code▯ sound effects . . .	
2. Scrambled screen quickly resolves to the basic message of the piece — a prime attribute of submarines. Screen resolves to . . .	
3. A series of video boxes with Submarine Force personnel all saying ▯STEALTH▯ in unison as the word ▯STEALTH▯ is ghosted over their pictures. Fades to . . .	

Description	Visuals
4. Army mules in huddle with periscope ▯watching▯ . . . cut to . . .	
5. Periscope view from inside huddle as the ▯stealthy▯ submarine gathers information on the next play . . . cut to . . .	
6. William Goat, the newest 1120, watching through the periscope . . .	

Description	Visuals
7. Cut to the Army Mules and Navy Goats lined up for the big play . . .	
8. The play begins . . .	
9. . . . a long pass down the field . . .	

The Finished Storyboard

Before the animators work on all the final details of their characters and the scenes, a finished storyboard is created. This shows the entire piece frame by frame. It also includes final descriptions of the action and dialogue. Once this storyboard is complete, everyone has a good idea of what the characters must do in each and every scene.

Top and left: *A finished storyboard for the "spirit piece."*

The final story-board includes a running description of action, dialogue, and sounds.

Description	Visuals
10. Caught by the star mule with an apparent clear field to the goal line . . . but wait . . . just in the nick of time	
11. William Goat, our 1120 hero, surfaces the boat . . . and ▯Clang▯ the mule runs smack into the sail, the ball flies up into ▯Bills▯ arms . . . pull in on Bill and then cut to . . .	
12. A series of video windows with Submarine Force personnel surrounding Bill as they chant ▯Go Navy — Beat Army▯ with the words ghosted over the pictures	
The End	The End

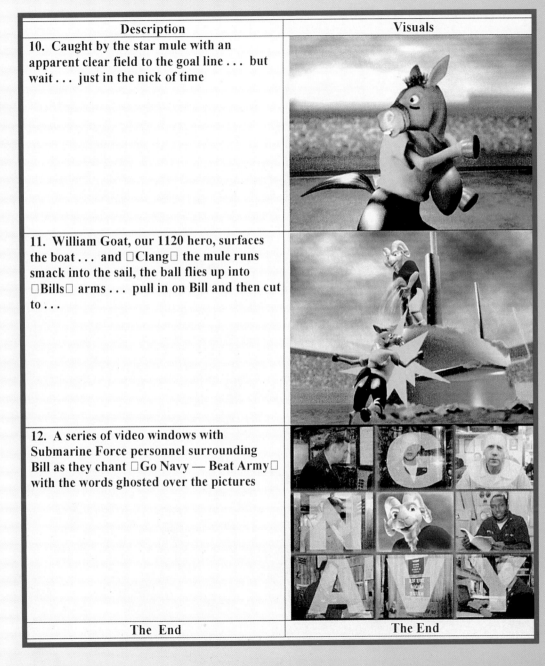

Special Sequences

Sometimes, one particular scene needs an unusual amount of work. If a scene has a complicated "sequence," (series of actions), it may be assigned to an animator whose only job is to work on that sequence. In the Navy piece, a submarine breaks through the football field in the middle of the game. To do the animation, Chris was asked to create these few seconds. He studied photos and drawings of submarines. He even found some old movie footage of a real sub breaking through some ice. He used this as the basis for his sequence.

Opposite: Chris Conway works on the submarine sequence.

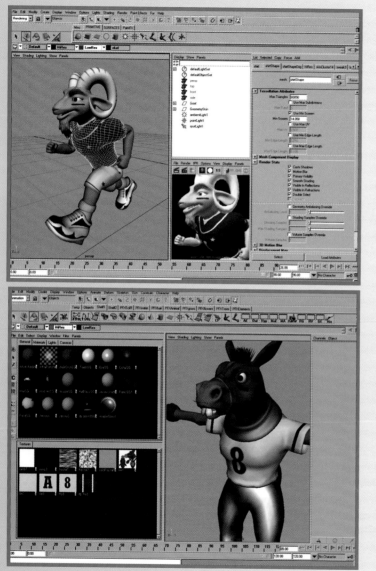

Details, Textures, and Light

As part of their final work, Gerardo and Erik design and program all the minor details for their characters. These include skin, hair, and clothing colors, and textures. They also decide what kind of lighting will be used in each scene. With the help of the computer, they can make their characters appear to be lighted by sunlight, moonlight, a spotlight, or a light on the ground—just about any kind of light.

Top and left: *The computer's software allows the animators to choose from a wide selection of colors, textures, and lighting for every character and scene.*

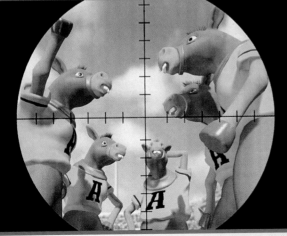

In this scene, the light is coming from above, like sunlight. The computer knows that this will create a shiny reflection on the football and a shadow on the goat's face.

Inset: Here, the characters are lighted from above, but the viewer sees them from below.

23

Adding Sound

When a piece is nearly done, a rough version of the 30 seconds goes to the sound department. Here, a skilled sound and recording engineer will add all the sounds and dialogue that will be heard.

Sound designer Curt Ramm prepares the sound board for recording.

The sound engineer starts with a list of sound effects and dialogue that must be included. He plans how each sound element will be recorded. In doing this, the sound engineer also "designs" the sounds that are used. He decides, for instance, if a character banging into the submarine makes a "hollow clang" or a "muffled thud." For every sound, a decision must be made.

Every sound must be recorded in exactly the right way. If the wrong sound is used, the viewer will not "believe" the action.

25

Sound Effects

Not every sound needs to be recorded fresh. Most sound departments have a large collection of pre-taped sound effects. These collections may include everything from the sound of shattering glass to dogs barking to trains whistling. When a sound person needs a sound, he or she will first go to the "sound library" to find one that works.

Sounds that are not available in the sound library need to recorded in a studio. The sound engineer plans and supervises these recordings to make sure the finished sounds are just right.

Left: Sound boards have hundreds of buttons and settings that create different recording effects. ***Opposite:*** Curt works with actor Chad Kelly to record the "eee-aw" of a mule braying.

"Layers" of Sound

When all the sound elements are collected, the sound designer adds "layers" of sound to each scene. The sound is done in "layers" because, in real life, there are often many sounds going on at once.

Top and left: Curt creates layers of sound for the football game in the "spirit piece."

Opposite: The video plays as the sound recordings show up on a separate monitor. This helps Curt adjust levels as he goes.

The Navy piece takes place in a huge football stadium. In the background of every scene is the noise of thousands of fans. There is also the game's announcer, and all the sounds made by the players. To these sounds, dialogue is added, along with special sounds made by the action being shown.

Final Touches

As the sound elements are finished, the final touches are placed on the animation. The piece is ready when the final soundtrack is added to the final version of the action.

Before the videotape of the piece is sent to the television network for broadcast, Lt. Scott Miller of the U.S. Navy comes for a viewing. When the tape is over, Lt. Miller is all smiles. He is sure it will be exactly what the Navy wants. And he knows that, even though it will only appear on national television for a brief 30 seconds, it is a "spirit piece" that will make both the U.S. Navy Submarine Force and the people in Sonalyst's animation department very proud of all the hard work that went into the finished product.

Top and left: Frames from the final version of the "spirit piece."

Left: *Lt. Miller (left) gets his first viewing of the "spirit piece," along with Producer Don LaForce (center) and animators Erik Paynter and Gerardo Orioli.*
Below: *A frame from the final version.*

Want to see the finished "spirit piece" as it ran on network television? Visit our web site at:
www.blackbirch.com

Glossary

Anatomy the way the body of a person or animal is put together.

Brainstorm when people get together and share ideas on a topic.

Budget a plan for how money will be spent.

Dialogue conversation, especially in a television commercial, movie, play, or book.

Mapped planned something out.

Realism the picturing of people and things as they really appear.

Supervise to be in charge of, watch over, or direct a group of people.

For More Information

Books

Baker, Christopher W. *Let There Be Life!: Animating With the Computer*. New York, NY: Walker & Co., 1997.

Kalbag, Asha. *Computer Graphics & Animation* (Computer Guides). Tulsa, OK: EDC Publications, 1999.

Smith, A. *The Usborne Complete Book of Drawing*. Tulsa, OK: Educational Development Center, 1994.

Waters, Kate. *Movies* (Scholastic Discovery Boxes). New York, NY: Scholastic Trade, 1996.

Web Site
Sonalysts, Inc.
Find out more about computer animation done by Sonalysts Studios–**www.sonalysts.com**.

Index

Animators, 3, 4, 5, 9, 10, 11, 14, 17, 18, 21, 31
Artists, 4
Characters, 3, 4, 10, 11, 12, 13, 14, 15, 16, 17, 18, 22, 23, 25
Commercials, 3, 4, 6, 8
Connecticut, 4
Drawing, 15

Football, 6, 21, 23, 28, 29
Goats, 10, 12, 13, 23
Grid, 17
"Layers," 28
Lighting, 15, 22, 23
Movement, 16
Movies, 3, 8
Mules, 10, 12, 13, 16, 26
"Plotting," 16

Producer, 7, 8, 31
"Sequence," 21
Sonalysts Studios, 4, 5, 6, 7, 10, 30
Sound, 24, 25, 26, 28, 29, 30
Sound board, 24, 26
"Sound library," 26
"Spirit piece," 6, 18, 30, 31

Storyboard, 9, 18, 19
Studio, 26
Submarine, 6, 21, 25, 30
Television, 3, 4, 8
U.S. Army, 6, 10
U.S. Navy, 6, 7, 10, 12, 21, 29, 30
Writers, 8